SUSHI & SASHIMI

Colophon

© 2002 published by Rebo Productions b.v., Lisse, The Netherlands

Internet: www.rebo-publishers.com - e-mail: info@rebo-publishers.com

Production, design and lay-out: Minkowsky, agency for graphic design, Enkhuizen, The Netherlands

Original recipes and photos: R&R Publishing Pty. Ltd.

Translation and adaptation: American Pie, London, UK and Sunnyvale, California

Cover design: Minkowsky, agency for graphic design, Enkhuizen, The Netherlands

ISBN 90 366 1481 3

SUSHI & SASHIMI

the secrets of the sushi chef as a guide to
creative cooking

REBO
PUBLISHERS

Foreword

It's a mystery how something as basic as sushi appear to be so complicated. If you have no experience with sushi, you may feel slightly intimidated.

After all, you're confronted with another language, different customs, and an enormous array of options in combining rice and fish. Consider blocks of rice with all sorts of seafood delicacies and small seaweed "boats." Sashimi may also sound too exotic to consider making yourself.

Your friends will probably be unable to help you. Some will say they don't like sushi and sashimi, particularly those who have never tried it, while some will be so enthusiastic about anago (conger eel) and uni (sea urchin) that it will be difficult for them to help a novice make a less exotic choice.

When you come "eye to fin" with your first sushi and sashimi experience, you have no idea what's in store for you. But don't fret. All you need is some more information and an open mind. This book offers a multitude of tips to help you navigate these new waters. With this book as your guide, you'll quickly learn how to prepare sushi and sashimi and how to eat it.

Abbreviations

tbsp = tablespoon

tsp = teaspoon

g = gram

kg = kilogram

fl oz = fluid ounce

lb = pound

oz = ounce

ml = milliliter

l = liter

°C = degree Celsius

°F = degree Fahrenheit

Where three measurements are given,

the first is the American liquid

measure.

Contents

Japan is an island nation. Its surrounding seas are warmed by the Kurashio, the plankton-rich Japan Current, which is rich in a variety of fish and shellfish. The islands themselves are mountainous, and what little arable land exists is terraced and carefully cultivated with rice and a number of other crops. Japan has always fed its population from the sea and the rice fields. Its cuisine emphasizes what nature has to offer. Sushi, the combination of raw fish and seasoned rice that seems to be so exotic to foreigners, is an extremely logical food in Japan.

Sushi began centuries ago in Japan as a method of preserving fish. Sushi supposedly originated in Southeast Asia. Cleaned, raw fish were pressed between layers of salt and weighted with a stone. After a few weeks, the stone was removed and replaced with a light cover, and a few months later the fermented fish and rice were considered to be ready to eat. Some Tokyo restaurants still serve this original style of sushi made from freshwater carp. This dish is called narezushi.

Origin of sushi

Narezushi has such a strong flavor that it obscures the identity of the fish. At first, it may be difficult to appreciate the dish.

It was not until the eighteenth century that a clever chef named Yohei decided to forego fermentation and serve sushi in something resembling its present-day form. It became very popular. Two different styles were created, the Kansai style, from the city of Osaka in the Kansai region and the Edo style, from the city of Tokyo, which was then called Edo. Osaka has always been the commercial capital of Japan, and the rice merchants there developed sushi that consisted primarily of seasoned rice mixed with other ingredients, from which decorative, edible packages were formed. Tokyo, located on a bay that was rich in fish and shellfish at the time, produced nigiri-sushi, featuring a selected piece of seafood on a small bed of seasoned rice. Although the ornamental sushi from the Kansai region is still very popular, foreigners are most familiar with nigiri-sushi.

Rice tub (hangiri)

The hangiri is used to give the vinegared rice its perfect texture and gloss. The tub is made of cypress wood bound with copper hoops, but any wooden or plastic container can be used as well.

Spatula (shamoji)

A shamoji is used to turn and spread sushi rice while cooling it. Traditionally, the spatula is a symbol of the housewife's position in the household. You can use an ordinary wooden or plastic spoon instead.

Fan (uchiwa)

The uchiwa is used to remove liquid and stimulate evaporation to get the proper texture and flavor of sushi rice. Originally, this fan was made of bamboo ribs covered with paper or silk. If no fan is available, a piece of cardboard or a magazine can be used instead.

Bowl

A large bowl with a lid is needed to store the cooked sushi rice to keep it warm until you make the sushi.

Basic necessities

Chopping board (manaita)

The manaita is essential. Traditionally made of wood, many people nowadays prefer chopping boards made of rubber or resin because they are easier to keep clean.

Chopsticks (saibashi)

Basically, there are two types of chopsticks. Long chopsticks, which are often made of metal, can be used to cook and lift food with practice. You eat with the shorter chopsticks.

Tweezers

You can use tweezers to extract small bones from the fish. A set of large tweezers with straight ends is preferred over the smaller type that is used in the bathroom. Tweezers are available at the fish market or at specialty stores.

Rolling mat (makisu)

The makisu is made of bamboo woven together with cotton string. This mat is used to make rolled-up sushi.

Knives

The only way to get beautifully cut surfaces is to use a good quality steel knife. Use whetstones and sharpen the blades yourself. Good Japanese knives are an outgrowth of forging the Japanese sword, which is world-famous for its sharpness. The knives are a chef's most valuable possession and sushi chefs always have a wet cloth on hand to wipe the blades to keep their knives clean as they work. The basic types appear below.

Cleavers (deba-bocho)

These are large, heavy knives with a triangular blade to cut through bone.

Vegetable knives (nakiri-bocho) These are lighter than cleavers and the blade is rectangular in shape.

Fish knives (sashimi-bocho) Sashimi-bocho are long and slender. The pointed type is most popular in Osaka, while the blunt type is most popular in Tokyo. They are excellent for filleting and slicing fish and perfect for slicing rolled-up sushi.

Vinegar

Sugared water or any alcoholic beverage left standing long enough becomes acidic and turns into vinegar. In Japan, vinegar is made from rice, the grain from which saké is brewed. Vinegar has the power to alter proteins and destroy bacteria. Adding sugar to sushi rice prevents the acidic vinegar taste from being too dominant.

Soy sauce

Soy sauce is popular the world over and is known by many names. Japanese soy sauce, rather than the darker and richer Chinese variety, is more popular among sushi-lovers. Soy sauce is highly recommended as a natural fermented food and is better than salt, sugar, or synthetic seasonings. The sauce is essential in most traditional Japanese dishes, including sushi, sukiyaki, and noodles. An open bottle of soy sauce should be stored in a cool, dark dry place or refrigerated.

Pickled ginger (gari or shoga)

Ginger is eaten to refreshen your mouth between two pieces of sushi. A lot of ginger is not necessary, a small amount should be sufficient for a number of rolls. Pickled ginger can be purchased at Japanese grocery stores, but you can also make it yourself.

Ingredients

Nori (seaweed)

After harvesting, the seaweed is dried, toasted and sold in standard sheet sizes (7x8 in/17.5x20cm). Once the sealed cellophane wrapper or plastic bag has been opened, nori should be eaten immediately or stored in a sealed container in a dry, cool, dark place to preserve its crispness. Nori is rich in vitamins A, B_{12}, and D.

Strips of nori are used with nigiri-sushi when the top layer, e.g. omelet and tofu, may slide off the rice. Cut a strip of nori around ½ in/1.25cm wide and wrap it around the top layer and the rice to hold it in place.

Tezu

This is a bowl, half filled with sushi vinegar and half filled with water. It is used to make sushi rice and keep top layers more manageable.

Saké

Sake is a colorless, brewed alcoholic beverage, made from rice, officially called rice beer. The bouquet is a bit robust, with subtle undertones. It has a mildly sweet taste and a dry aftertaste. Saké should be stored in a cool, dark place before opening and in the refrigerator after opening. The beverage is very popular in Japan, traditionally served before eating sushi. Saké should be served warm.

Mirin

Mirin is known as sweet saké. Usually, it is only used as flavoring. Sweet sherry is a good substitute if mirin is unavailable.

Daikon

Daikon is a Japanese white radish, which is available fresh from oriental grocery stores in lengths ranging from 6in/15cm to 2ft/60cm. Daikon keeps for several weeks in the refrigerator. It is cut in thin slices and eaten with sashimi or used as a replacement for nori seaweed. You can add chopped daikon to soy sauce for a different texture and flavor.

Tofu

Tofu is a block of soybean coagulant that looks like a spongy white cheese. It is sold fresh in the supermarket and keeps for a number of days in the refrigerator if stored in fresh water. Tofu is often used in nigiri-sushi as a replacement for sushi rice or as a top layer over the rice.

Sushi rice

With sushi, the rice is as important as the fish. It takes years to learn to make the perfect sushi rice. There are various ways to do this, but you will find instructions for a generally accepted and uncomplicated method for making the rice on page 50.

Flat slicing technique

Sashimi slicing technique

Slanted slicing technique

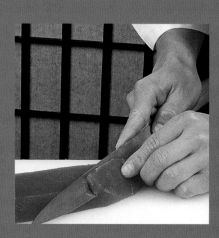

The following are five basic methods for slicing sashimi and sushi. A very sharp knife is essential.

Flat slicing technique (hira giri) This is the most popular form, which is suitable for every filleted fish. Hold the fish firmly and slice straight through until you are left with slices around ⅛–½ inch/1–2mm thick and 2 in/5cm wide, depending on the size of the fillet.

Wire slicing (ito zukeri) Although this technique can be applied for every small fish, it is particularly suitable for squid. Cut the squid straight in ⅛ inch/1mm slices, then cut the slices lengthwise in ⅛ in/1mm wide slices.

Slicing blocks (kazu giri) This slicing technique is often used for tuna. Cut the tuna as described with the flat slicing technique and then cut it in ½ in/1.25cm blocks.

Paper-thin slices (usu zukuri) Place a whitefish fillet such as sea bream or snapper on a flat surface and hold the fish firmly with one hand, while you slice it at an angle in nearly transparent slices.

Slanted slicing technique (sori giri) This is an ideal slice for a sushi top layer. Begin with a rectangular piece of fish such as salmon or tuna, cut a triangle off a corner, then cut off pieces around ⅛–½ in/1–2mm thick.

Many Japanese are also unaware of the correct way to eat sushi. By eating it as explained here, you will take full advantage of the taste and experience of this fantastic food. There are two ways to eat sushi.

Method 1

Place the sushi on its side and lift both the top layer and the rice with chopsticks or your fingers (thumb, index finger, and middle finger).

Dip the end of the top layer, not the rice, in the soy sauce.

Place the sushi in your mouth with the top layer directly on your tongue.

Method 2

Take some pickled ginger and dip it in the soy sauce.

Apply soy sauce to the top layer, with the ginger as a brush.

Place the sushi in your mouth with the top layer directly on your tongue.

How to eat sushi

There is no set order in which the various types of sushi are eaten, but the nori-wrapped pieces should be eaten first, since the crispness of nori does not last long once it comes in contact with moist rice.

Do not soak the sushi in too much soy sauce. The rice will fall apart and the taste of soy will dominate. The same applies for wasabi and pickled ginger. Be modest, otherwise the taste of the topping and the rice will be concealed rather than complemented.

At today's sushi counters, you can drink whatever you like with your sushi, but saké and green tea are the most appropriate drinks. Saké is served warm and before you eat–not during or after. The tea, however, is served throughout the meal. Green tea is essential for the full enjoyment of sushi. It removes the aftertaste and freshens the mouth for the next serving.

Nutrition experts regard sushi as a well-balanced, healthy food because it contains many nutrients, including minerals and vitamins that would otherwise be partially lost while cooking.

Rice

Rice is an excellent source of complex carbohydrates and nutritional fibers. Nutritional fibers play an important role in digestion, while carbohydrates deliver slow-release energy, which therefore lasts longer. Rice is also a good source of niacin, protein, thiamine, and iron.

Fish and seafood

Seafood is low in calories, fewer than in the leanest chicken and meat. It provides an excellent source of high-quality proteins and minerals, including iodine, zinc, potassium, and phosphorus. Fish and seafood are also rich in vitamins, particularly those from the B complex. The small quantity of fat in fish is rich in omega-3 fatty acids, which makes fish good for the heart. Omega-3 fatty acids from fish can prevent the formation of blood clots and clogging of the arteries, thereby reducing the risk of heart attack.

Health and sushi

Nori

Seaweed is an excellent source of iodine, calcium, and iron, all three of which are important in maintaining a healthy blood and bone structure. It also contains a lot of vitamin B_{12}. This makes sushi a valuable source of this vitamin, which is otherwise present only in animal products.

Soybeans

Soybeans provide the best proteins of all legumes. They are used to make tofu, soy sauce, and miso. Since soybeans contain starch, they have a high fat content in the form of polyunsaturated oil. They also provide nutritional fibers, vitamins of the B group and a number of minerals.

Wasabi

Wasabi is an excellent source of vitamin C.

Preparation

Insert a 6in/15cm bamboo skewer through the shrimp to prevent curling.

Place the shrimp in a saucepan with 2 cups/16fl oz/500ml boiling water and salt and vinegar and let it simmer for 2-3 minutes.

Remove the shrimp and place them in ice-cold water. Add cold water, if necessary, to ensure that the shrimp are well cooled. Rotate the skewers to remove the shrimp.

Peel the shrimp by removing the legs and the head, but leave the tip of the tail intact.

Make a lengthwise notch in the back of the shrimp, then remove the intestinal vein from the body.

Place the knife in the leg side of the shrimp and open it like a butterfly.

Soak the shrimp 20 minutes in salt water. Then place in a bowl with vinegar water and soak for another 20 minutes.

Prepare nigiri-sushi as described on page 52.

Ingredients

10 jumbo shrimp (scampi)

½ tsp/2.5g salt

½ tsp/2.5ml vinegar

1¼ cups/10oz/280g sushi rice

2 tsp/10g wasabi paste

10 thin wooden skewers

vinegar water

2 cups/16fl oz/500ml water

1 cup/8fl oz/250ml rice vinegar

Nigiri-sushi with shrimp (ebi)

Nigiri-sushi

The word sushi usually refers to "nigiri-sushi," hand-formed

sushi that is usually served in sushi restaurants. Nigiri-sushi rep-

resents the food from Tokyo and many varieties contain seafood

or fish. This may have to do with the fact that the city has

always been rich in all sorts of seafood.

nigiri-sushi

Preparation

Proceed with the techniques used in preparing nigiri-sushi.

Note

Various types of tuna are available. Take a look at a fish market and inquire at the fishmonger. These types of tuna are recommended.

Blue fin tuna: most Japanese consider this type to be the best fish in the tuna family.

Large-eyed tuna: this type is also well-known, and is second most expensive in the Japanese market after the blue fin tuna.

Yellow-fin tuna: an extremely common tropical type of tuna. Freshly refrigerated, it is flown to Japan by plane, although the sashimi market outside Japan is now using increasingly larger quantities.

Albacore (white tuna): this tuna is highly suitable for sashimi, but is quite calorie-rich. Albacore is often called the 'chicken of the sea' due to its mild chicken flavor after it has been prepared.

Nigiri-sushi with tuna (maguru)

Ingredients

12 oz/350g tuna fillet

1¼ cups/10oz/280g sushi rice

1 tbsp/15g wasabi

nigiri-sushi

Preparation

Take a piece of thinly-sliced salmon fillet between the thumb and index finger of your left hand. Make a ball of around 1 tbsp/15g sushi rice (somewhat smaller than a golf ball). Dab a small amount of wasabi in the middle of the salmon with your index finger. Place the rice on the salmon. Press on the rice with your left thumb, this will leave a slight imprint in the ball. Press the bottom and the top of the rice between the index finger and thumb of your right hand. Push in the surface of the rice with your right index finger. Close your left hand and turn to the right.
The top layer should now be facing upward. Place your index finger and middle finger on the top layer. Close your left hand and raise it slightly. Turn clockwise with your right index finger and thumb. Push in both sides and repeat steps 7-11 twice or three times.

Nigiri-sushi with salmon (saké)

Ingredients

12 oz/350g salmon fillet

1¼ cups/10oz/280g sushi rice

1 tbsp/15g wasabi

Tip

Most beginners use too much rice. Take less than you think you will need. Most beginners put too much water on their hands. Use only a small amount.

nigiri-sushi

Preparation

Cut off the head of the octopuses and turn the mollusks inside out.
Sprinkle 2 tbsp/30g of salt on the octopuses and brush this into the meat, to
removing the sliminess. Prepare a large pan of boiling water, add 2 tbsp/30g of
salt, the sushi vinegar, and the green tea. Cook the octopuses 8–10 minutes.
Remove the octopuses from the boiling water and place them in a pan of cold
water, with 2 tbsp/30g of salt and 4 tbsp/60ml of sushi vinegar. Let the octopuses
stand for 10 minutes. Cut the octopuses into thin slices and prepare nigiri-sushi as
described on page 52.

Nigiri-sushi with octopus (tako)

Ingredients

2 medium-sized octopuses (around 1 lb/450g each), cleaned

6 tbsp/90g salt

4 tbsp/60ml sushi vinegar

2 tbsp/30g Japanese green tea (ocha)

2 cups/1 lb/450g sushi rice

15–20 strips nori

Nigiri-sushi with yellowtail (boh-sushi)

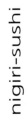

Preparation

The easiest type of sushi to prepare – which is also made in all Japanese kitchens – is chirashi-sushi or sprinkle sushi. Chirashi-sushi is sushi rice with other ingredients, which are mixed into the rice or placed on top of it. Chirashi-sushi without seafood is often found in lunchboxes. The dish is popular for picnics and is often sold at railroad stations. Stations are even known for this type of food and for their unique luncheon packaging. Here, too, the sushi variations are nearly endless. The rice can also be flavored with various interesting ingredients such as chopped vegetables, sesame seed, pieces of tofu, slivered fresh and pickled ginger, crumbled nori, and various sauces.

Chirashi-sushi

Suggestions for top layers

tuna, shrimp

omelet, octopus

salmon, unagi eel

yellowtail, bonito

avocado, tofu

crab, vegetables

nigiri-sushi

Preparation

Cut the tofu into slices.

Mix the ginger, the green onion (scallion) and the soy sauce.

Add the ingredients for the top layer.

Place the top layer on the tofu and bind it together with a strip of nori.

Place the mixed ginger on top and serve the sushi.

Note

The garnishing already contains soy. Therefore, a bowl of soy and wasabi is unnecessary.

Ingredients

¾ lb/340g tofu (to replace sushi rice)

selection of various types of fish and vegetables

grated ginger

minced scallion

½ tsp /2.5g soy sauce

15 – 20 strips nori

Dynamite roll (spicy tuna)

Preparation

Slice the omelet, the cucumber, the avocado and the eel in strips of

around 1⅛ x ½ x 3in/1x2x75mm long.

Follow the instructions on page 56 to make the thick rolls.

Preparation

Peel the shrimp and remove the intestinal vein. Cut the shrimp in half lengthwise.

Prepare California rolls as described on page 56.

Variation

Clean a large carrot, cut it into thick strips and blanch it. Blanch ⅓ cup/3½oz/100g

spinach leaves in salt water, rinse it with cold water, let it drain and shake dry.

Cut 4oz/125g fresh salmon fillet in slices 1in/2.5cm thick and marinate in mirin.

Prepare the California roll as described.

California roll (ura maki sushi)

Ingredients

4 sheets nori seaweed, 1 tbsp/5g wasabi

3 cups/1lb 10oz/750g sushi rice

3 tbsp/45ml Japanese mayonnaise, 4-8 pieces coral seaweed

4 medium shrimp or surimi (crabsticks)

1 ripe avocado, peeled, pitted, and sliced

1 cucumber, cut into thin strips

4 tsp/20g flying-fish roe

maki-sushi

Preparation

Prepare the filling for the rolls. Cut the salmon, avocado, and cucumber to the proper length.

Proceed with the rolls as described on page 58.

Note

You can adjust the filling according to seasonal availability and your taste. Take what you like and what is available. For example, sesame seed, salmon roe, or dried bonito flakes are a tasty alternative to flying-fish roe.

Ingredients

4 sheets nori seaweed

3 cups/1lb 10oz/750g sushi rice

4 tsp/20g flying-fish roe

½ tsp/2.5g wasabi

8oz/250g salmon fillet

1 ripe avocado

1 cucumber

Inside-out rolls (sakamaki)

Preparation

Place a sheet of nori on a bamboo mat. Distribute a third of the sushi rice over the nori. Place a sheet of nori on the first layer. Distribute another third of the sushi rice over the nori. Prepare the sushi roll as described on page 56. Cut the roll into four pieces lengthwise. Place the last sheet of nori on the bamboo mat and distribute the remaining rice over it. Turn the nori and place it on a cloth, as described under Sakamaki (page 58). Place four quarters of the pre-sliced roll next to each other, place the omelet in the center, and start rolling.

Roll it up and make a square, press the grated egg yoke against the sides, and cut the roll into four equal pieces.

Square rolls (shikai maki)

Ingredients

3 sheets nori seaweed

1¼ cups/10oz/380g sushi rice

sushi omelet cut in ½ inch/2cm squares

kimi oboro (grated hard-boiled egg yolk)

maki-sushi

Preparation

Temaki-sushi was originally a meal for busy chefs. Since they had the ingredients at hand, but lacked the time to make sushi for themselves, they made it'with "hand-rolled sushi." Temaki is a type of sushi that comes in a cone form. Temaki is a good way to experiment with ingredients such as cooked chicken, raw or cooked beef, smothered in tasty sauces, if desired. These sushi are quick and easy to make and are very tasty, even with an inexpensive filling.

If you cannot find any toasted sheets of nori seaweed, toast them yourself. Lightly toast only one side of each sheet of nori around 30 seconds over a gas flame. The taste is somewhat diminished if both sides are toasted. You can also toast the sheets in a dry frying pan on low heat until you can smell the aroma. The nori will be crispy and dark green after frying.

You can finely chop scraps of toasted sheets of nori seaweed and use as seasoning or as a snack. If you make temaki-sushi with semi-liquid ingredients, it is best to place the rice underneath and the filling on top.

Fresh daikon sprigs are popular ingredients for temaki-sushi and maki-sushi. Daikon sprigs are fairly spicy and pungent. They are well suited for omelet sushi. Daikon sprigs are available in oriental stores and can often be found at the grocery store or at the market where they are also known as mooli. You can also grow daikon at home from seed. Small temaki-sushi is perfect as a starter because it is easy to eat with the hands.

Temaki-sushi

Ingredients

10 sheets nori seaweed, cut in half

2¼ cups/550g/1lb 4 oz sushi rice

wasabi

Note

As a special variant or if you do not have any sheets of nori seaweed on hand, tamaki-sushi can even be rolled in lettuce, particularly in Romaine lettuce or iceberg lettuce. Lettuce makes for a light, refreshing roll.

Suggestions for the filling

slices of tuna, spicy tuna

tempura shrimp, teriyaki head

smoked shrimp, surimi (crabsticks), unagi eel fillet

pickled whiting or yellowtail sashimi, flying-fish roe, salmon roe, or sea urchin roe

omelet, cucumber, avocado, smoked salmon (or other smoked fish)

You can use Japanese mayonnaise or cream cheese instead of wasabi.

maki-sushi

This chapter will tell you everything you need to know for making perfect sushi at home.

Preparation

Rice for sushi should be somewhat firmer in texture than for other dishes. You need about 1 cup/8oz/250g of cooked rice for each roll. It is better to make too much rice than not enough. Each sushi rice recipe is different, but they are all good. You may find a recipe on a bottle of rice vinegar, on a package of sushi rice, or on the nori package.

Most recipes suggest that you rinse the raw rice until the water runs clear. However, this is not absolutely necessary. The most important reason for rinsing rice is to remove the talc from the rice. Since most rice today is coated with cornstarch instead of talc, rinsing can be omitted. Often, the recipe also suggests that you drain the rice for 30 – 60 minutes in a colander or zaru. The choice is up to you. In any case, you should always use Japanese, short-grained, sushi rice. Wash the rice until the water is clear, if desired. Mix the rice and water in a saucepan and let the rice stand for 30 minutes. Bring the rice and water to a boil. Lower the heat and let the rice simmer for 10 minutes. Turn off the burner and let the rice steam for 20 minutes. Make sushi vinegar (mix all ingredients in a pan and heat until they dissolve). Distribute the rice over a cookie sheet, sprinkle with sushi vinegar. Mix everything as if you are cutting it. Use a fan to cool the rice to body temperature.

Preparing sushi rice

Ingredients

4 cups/2lb/900g Japanese sushi rice

4 cups/1¾ pints/1l water

For the sushi vinegar

½ cup/4fl oz/125ml rice vinegar

4 tbsp/60g sugar

1 tsp/5g salt

½ tsp/2.5ml soy sauce

Right: Preparing sushi rice

(shari or sushi meshi)

1

Rinse a Japanese wooden rice tub (hangiri) or a flat wooden plate with cold water before you scoop in the hot rice.

2

Add the sushi vinegar to the rice. Pour the vinegar over the rice on a large wooden spoon so that it is evenly distributed.

3

Mix the vinegar with the rice, but do not flatten the rice.

4

Use a fan to cool the rice to room temperature.

techniques

1

Prepare the tezu, which is half-water and half-sushi vinegar. Moisten the fingers and palms of the hand with the tezu.

2

Take a piece of fish with one hand and a handful of prepared sushi rice with the other. Mold the rice in the shape of a block.

Preparation

The most important aspect of nigiri-sushi is the balance between the top layer and the rice. You form the sushi with the hand by carefully molding the ingredients. You need a cutting board, a sharp knife and vinegar water (tezu) to rinse off the fingers, the fish and the prepared rice.

Making nigiri-sushi

3

Hold the piece of fish in one hand and spread a small amount of wasabi on the fish.

4

Place the rice on the piece of fish in your hand. Use your thumb and lightly press on the rice to create a hollow.

5

Use the index finger of the other hand to press on the rice, flattening it.

6

Turn the sushi, so the fish is on top and use the thumb and middle finger to mold the rice.

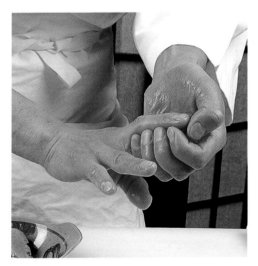

7

Hold your fingers in your hand as illustrated and cover the fish and the rice. Press carefully around the sushi. Repeat steps 5-7 twice more.

8

If all goes well, you now have a piece of sushi, with fish covering the firm rice.

1

Cut a sheet of nori seaweed in half length-
wise. Use two pieces to make the sushi rolls.
Place the shiny side of the nori on the mat.
Moisten your hands with some tezu.

2

Take a handful of rice from the rice tub.
Distribute the rice evenly over the nori.

Thin sushi rolls (hosomaki)

3

Spread the desired quantity of wasabi on the
rice with your index finger. Begin on one side
and distribute it from the middle to the other
side.

4

Place the tuna strips in the center of the rice,
on the wasabi. Lift the edge of the bamboo
mat.

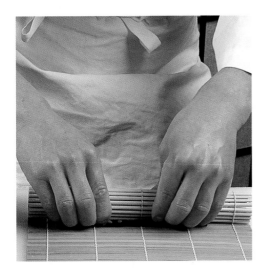

5

Hold the mat and the filling with the fingers of both hands. Roll the mat and the nori over the filling and make sure that all ingredients are evenly pressed.

6

Continue rolling, but use somewhat more pressure to make the rice compact. Repeat the last step if necessary, so that the rice from the entire roll is pressed firmly and evenly.

7

Remove the roll from the mat and place it on a cutting board. Cut the roll in half.

8

You can usually make six pieces from a roll. Place the two halves next to one another and cut each half into three pieces.

techniques

1

Place one sheet of nori with the shiny side on the bamboo mat, moisten your hands with some tezu and take a handful of sushi rice.

2

Distribute the rice evenly over the nori.

Thick sushi rolls (futomaki)

3

Apply the desired quantity of wasabi to the center of the rice.

4

Add some Japanese mayonnaise in the same way.

5

Add the filling of your choice, place it in the
middle, and on the wasabi and mayonnaise.

6

Roll the mat over the ingredients to around
1 in/2.5cm from the outer edge of the nori.

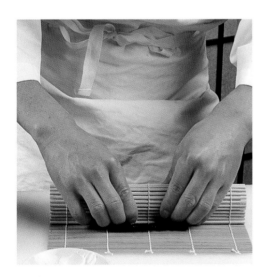

7

Lift the mat and roll it forward again so the
edges of the nori adhere while you apply some
pressure to tighten the roll.

8

Use a sharp knife to cut the entire roll in half,
place the two halves next to one another, and
cut each half into three pieces. You can make
six pieces from each roll.

techniques

1

Place a sheet of nori on a bamboo mat and take a handful of rice.

2

Distribute the rice evenly over the nori. Then remove the nori and the rice from the mat and place them on a moist cloth.

Inside-out rolls (sakamaki)

3

Place the nori on the moist cloth and distribute the desired quantity of wasabi over the center of the nori.

4

Place the ingredients in the center of the nori.

5

Roll the mat over the ingredients to around
1in/2.5cm from the outer edge of the nori.

6

Lift the mat and roll it forward again so the
edges of the nori adhere while you apply some
pressure to tighten the roll.

7

Remove the finished roll from the mat and
place it on a platter. Slowly arrange the roe
around the roll until the rice is covered.

8

Use a sharp knife to cut the rolls in half, place
the two halves next to one another and cut
each half into three pieces. You can make six
pieces from each roll.

techniques

Temaki-sushi

1

Take a sheet of nori in one hand and a handful of rice, about as large as a golf ball, in the other.

2

Place the rice on one side of the sheet of nori and distribute it. Cover only half of the sheet of nori with the rice.

2

Add the water and the ice cubes to the yolk.

3

Use chopsticks or a fork to mix the egg yolk

and the cold water.

4

Add the flour to the egg-water mixture.

5

Mix the ingredients well until smooth.

techniques

Wash the fish and leave it wet, making it is easier to clean. Remove the scales with a knife. Begin with the tail and scrape toward the head.

Cut off the dorsal fin with a pair of scissors or remove both the back and anal fin by cutting along the sides of the fin with a sharp knife. Pull the fin toward the head to remove it.

Cut off the head behind the gill opening before boning or filleting. Use a sharp knife to cut open the stomach from the head until just above the anal fin. Remove the membranes, arteries, and intestines. Rinse the fish well.

Cut through the gills and open the outer gill with the thumb to retain the form of round fish. Insert a finger in the gill and take hold of the innermost gill. Pull carefully to remove the innermost gill and the intestines. Rinse the fish well.

Make a groove around the entire body, behind the gills, and the intestines just above the tail to clean the entire fish. Then make a cut in the back.

Use a sharp knife and, beginning at the tail, and separate the skin from the meat. Pull the knife toward the head while you hold the skin firmly with your other hand. Do not "saw" with the knife.

Place the fillet skin with the side toward the bottom and cut a small piece of meat from the skin close to the tail. Hold the fillet taut and pull a sharp knife along the skin.

Filleting

sashimi

Preparation

Clean the horse mackerel, remove the intestines, and fillet it
as described on page 67.

Cut the fillets with the "flat slicing technique" as described
on page 96.

Embellish the dish, if desired, with a rose made from a couple
of paper-thin pieces of the fish. Garnish with radish.

Ingredients

1 whole horse mackerel (approx. 2 lbs.)

grated radish for garnish

Note

Various types of horse mackerel are available, but the smaller types are tastier.

The large fish are often somewhat drier and blander in taste.

The horse mackerel has firm, white meat with a mild 'fish' taste and is an excellent, sometimes

somewhat undervalued fish to eat as sashimi.

Horse mackerel sashimi (shimaaji)

Preparation

Cut the tuna fillet with a straight slicing technique. Place the soy sauce, saké, and dried bonito in a saucepan, bring everything to a boil, and stir the mixture for 2 minutes. Press the tuna through a fine sieve and let it cool to room temperature. Spread the dipping sauce on small plates next to the tuna sashimi.

Note

If the fillet you bought has already been cut in a square, you can cut the fish for sashimi. If not, you need to buy a larger fillet and cut this to size yourself. You can use the scraps as tuna flakes.

Tuna sashimi (maguro)

Ingredients

12oz/350g sashimi-quality tuna fillet

Tosa Juya (dipping sauce)

3 tbsp/45ml soy sauce

2½ tsp/12.5ml saké

2½ tsp/12.5g dried bonito (katsuobushi)

sashimi

Preparation

Clean the snapper, remove the intestines, and fillet it as described on page 67.

Cut the fillets straight in paper-thin slices as described on page 13.

Arrange the grated carrot and chicory on the platter as garnish.

Ingredients

1 medium snapper (about 3½ lb/1.6kg)

grated carrot

chicory

Note

Snapper is one of the most valued edible fish. Although the snapper is very well known as a fish that is eaten warm, it is best used in sashimi style. Many Japanese restaurants serve it this way. Snapper has firm, white meat with a sweet to mild taste.

Snapper sashimi (tai)

sashimi

Preparation

If you buy an entire salmon, clean it, remove the intestines, and fillet it as described on page 67.

Cut away any visibly dark or bruised meat, and skin and "fatty" flesh. Using the straight slicing technique, cut the fillets in a block in the required number of pieces (you can chop up scraps of salmon, mix with wasabi, and use for sushi, if desired). Place the fillets on a platter and garnish with grated daikon.

Salmon sashimi (sake)

Ingredients

12oz/350g sashimi quality salmon or 1 whole salmon

grated radish

Note

The Atlantic salmon is valued as fish for the table, not only as sashimi, but in fried or broiled form as well. This type of salmon has a rich taste and firm, succulent meat.

sashimi

Preparation

Clean the bonito, remove the intestines, and fillet it as described on page 67.

Cut the fillets with a straight slicing technique (leave the skin on).

Place the fillets on a serving platter and garnish with grated ginger.

Ingredients

1 whole bonito (about 4½ lb/2kg)

½ tsp/2.5g ginger, grated

Note

Various types of bonito are available all over the world. The fish meat is flesh-colored and has a magnificent, coarse texture, and a rich taste.

If you buy fillets, choose firm, succulent, marbled meat.

The color is a good indicator for freshness. A freshly cut surface is very dull.

Bonito sashimi (katsuo)

Preparation

Clean the yellowtail, remove the intestines, and fillet it as described on page 67. Remove all bones and skin. Cut the fillets in fine strips as described on page 13. Mix the yellowtail, the ginger, and the green onions (scallions) and let the mixture stand for around 30 minutes to bring out the flavor.

Yellowtail sashimi (tatakin)

Ingredients

3 yellowtails

4 green onions (scallions), chopped, 1 tsp/5g ginger, grated

Note

The yellowtail is part of the pike-perch family from the Pacific Ocean and is popular in New Zealand and North America. Yellowtail is very popular in Japan for sashimi. The fillets are somewhat dry and fatty and moderately strong in taste.

sashimi

Preparation

Remove the heads to prepare the jumbo shrimp and save them for garnishing.

Remove the bottommost scale from the top of the tail.

Remove the meat and discard the scales, except for the bottom of the tail.

Place the scampi meat on a platter. Use the heads and tails as garnish.

Heat saké in a saucepan for the dipping sauce. Light it with a match after you have removed the pan from the flame and carefully shake the pan until the flame extinguishes. Let the saké cool.

Add the saké to the other ingredients and mix well. Pour the mixture in small bowls and serve with scampi or other sashimi.

Ingredients

8 scampi (fresh if possible, otherwise frozen)

Chirizu (spicy dipping sauce)

5 tsp/25ml sake, 3 tbsp/45g freshly grated daikon

2 green onions (scallions), cut in rings

3 tbsp/45ml soy sauce, 3 tbsp/45ml lemon juice

dash of togarashi (seven-spice powder)

Note

Jumbo shrimp are usually frozen on board the trawlers right after they are caught, making it much more difficult to find fresh specimens. They have delicious sweet meat and are ideal for sashimi. Many find them tastier than lobster.

Scampi sashimi (tenagaebi)

Preparation

If you purchase frozen lobster, let it thaw overnight in the refrigerator. Remove the head to save as garnish. Use poultry scissors to make a nice straight score in the tail shell.

Pull out the lobster meat. Fill the empty platter with grated daikon for the presentation. Cut the lobster into small sashimi slices. Place the meat on the daikon-filled tail and serve.

Lobster sashimi (ise ebi)

Ingredients

1 whole uncooked lobster

chicory, grated carrot, grated daikon

Note

Lobsters for sashimi can be bought live and killed just before serving.

This is the custom because of the Japanese obsession with absolute freshness.

Using chopsticks

Pick up the chopsticks and place them in your hand so that they are easy to use, while holding them higher up toward the thick side. Turn the points of the chopsticks before you serve yourself from a common dish. Unused chopsticks should be placed to the right of your plate.

Sushi etiquette

At the bar

The experienced sushi eater first orders a selection of sashimi to give the sushi chef the chance to show his best fish. Always ask the chef what he would recommend. Sashimi is eaten with chopsticks, not with the hands. When you are finished with the sashimi, ask for another soy dish. Wasabi should not be mixed in, since it has already been placed between the rice and the fish. You are now ready for the nigiri-sushi. Nigiri should be eaten with the hands, therefore do not waste time juggling with sticks. Dip the end briefly in the soy sauce and place the sushi with the fish side on your tongue. Do not bite into the piece, but place the entire piece in your mouth. The chef will look at your plate to see how you are progressing, not for your next choice. When you're finished, ask the waiter (not the chef) for the bill.

Sushi chefs are proud of their work and should be left a nice tip.

Poor manners

Do not ask for a knife. This would imply that the food is tough and cannot be eaten without a knife. Do not use chopsticks to pass food to someone else. This is compared to passing on the cremated bones of a deceased family member during a Japanese funeral.

Do not scrape rice from chopsticks. Do not eat all the rice in one go; try other dishes first. You should always eat the rice you have taken.

Try not to swing your chopsticks over the food while you're trying to decide what to eat.

Wasabi

Do not use too much wasabi. Wasabi numbs the palate and conceals the subtle flavor of fish if it is eaten raw.

background information

91

The chef, dressed in a smock with short sleeves and a brightly colored headband, performs magic with a ball of rice and the most magnificent pieces of bright orange salmon.

The waiter regularly comes along with a tray for the back tables. You see dark green, cone-shaped California rolls with fish and avocado, while other interesting rolls containing fresh tuna or cucumber serve as focal point.

After you have eaten, the chef or waiter will offer you a menu, usually with color photos and descriptions in English. You will also be offered something to drink, and you will be faced with your first – and most important – test. You are going to try saké.

The sushi bar

Saké is a Japanese wine, made from fermented rice, traditionally served with fish dishes. The beverage is strong, aromatic, and a little sweet. But a word of caution before you begin: an empty cup is considered rude, so your host or hostess will keep it filled. Turn the cup upside down if you have had enough.

There is no need to be concerned about your place setting. Since there are no knives and forks, you learn to eat with sticks or use your fingers. Both are acceptable. A small bottle of soy sauce (shoyu) and a shallow dish for mixing the sauce with a little wasabi (green horseradish paste) are on the table.

You also see a small serving of gari (ginger) at the edge of your plate.

These paper-thin slices are pink and pickled. They neutralize the previous taste sensation and prepare you for the next.

 See it as a reset button for your taste buds…

Chopsticks can be frustrating for novices. Just as you succeed in picking up a block of rice, you dip it in the sauce and the entire piece falls apart before it has reached your mouth. Try this: turn over the sushi and dip the fish side in your shoyu mixture. It is important to complement the taste of the fish, not the rice. Now you only have to decide what to order first. There is something for everyone.

Heir to the samurai tradition

The spirit of sushi has been transferred by the shokunin (the traditional master sushi chefs) over the centuries. The Japanese strongly believe in learning through apprenticeship. Before the student can even pick up a knife, he has to work in the kitchen, sweep the floors, wash the dishes, and perform other odd jobs for at least a number of years. It may take ten years of training to become a master and head chef.

The sushi chef is heir to the samurai tradition and holds the ideals of the samurai high–scholars and gentlemen with high personal standards and values and great self-discipline. They wear immaculate ghis and a headband with a knot, which show that they take their work very seriously.

Sushi is considered to be an art in a country in which cooking is highly regarded as a profession. It is an honor to become a sushi chef.

The sushi chef

Tools

Knives are as important to the sushi chef as the sword to a samurai. The chef's knives are made from carbon steel and are sharp enough to split a hair. A sushi chef has his own set of knives, which may cost a couple hundred dollars apiece. He sharpens them before and after use, cleans them after a couple of slices, wraps them, and stores them overnight in a safe place. In contrast to most knives, sushi knives are only sharpened on one side for a rapid, cleaner cut.

Anago (conger eel) – Anago or conger eel, a leaner version of the unagi, freshwater eel. It is always cooked first. It need not be accompanied by dipping sauce or wasabi, since it is served with a special mixture of sugar, soy sauce, and eel broth.

Glossary

Buzuguri – pieces of octopus.

Ebi (boiled shrimp) – Ebi are very popular on sushi menus because of their sweet, fresh taste. They are shrimp that are cooked in salt water, then peeled and butterflied, so that only the scale of the tail remains. They are usually eaten with wasabi and soy sauce.

Gari (sliced ginger) – Gari is a garnish that is used to refresh the mouth between two sushi servings. It is ginger root that is pickled in salt and sweet vinegar. For the best results when buying gari to make sushi, choose ginger with a smooth peel to make firm pieces.

Gunkan – Gunkan is called "battleship style" sushi. It is a type of nigiri-sushi that is made by binding a strip of seaweed around a ball of rice that is pressed flat so that ingredients can be placed on top. This is a simple way to serve fish roe and other small ingredients.

Hamachi (yellowtail) – Hamachi is a type of yellowtail. It is pale yellow, with a rich, soft, smoky taste. Sushi chefs consider the fish's tail and cheeks to be the best parts, which they often save and prepare for special customers.

Hira special – Cream cheese, cucumber, crab, avocado, salmon and tuna – this sushi is rolled inside out, with the rice on the outside.

Ikura (salmon roe) – This is a red, shiny ball-like sushi. The name ikura stems from ikra, a Russian word for roe or caviar. That is why ikura is sometimes used as red caviar in western cuisine and in sushi.

Kani (crab) – Kani is always served cooked and is an excellent choice for a beginning sushi-eater. The crab can be eaten in nigiri-sushi or wrapped in seaweed as in California rolls. Kani is real crabmeat, while kanikama is artificial crabmeat (surimi) that is sometimes used in certain types of sushi.

Kyuri – Cucumber wrapped in seaweed.

Maguro (tuna) – Maguro is the most popular dish sold in a sushi bar, due to its familiarity and its fresh, pure taste. Although there are many types of tuna, lean yellow-fin or blue-fin tuna meat are used for sushi. If you wish to try to roll it yourself, the chefs recommend experimenting with maguro-sushi in the winter, when the tuna is at its best.

Maki-sushi (rolled sushi) – A type of sushi made of rice, fish, and other ingredients by rolling a long seaweed roll and cutting it into small pieces. There are two types of maki-sushi rolls: hosomaki, a thin roll from which six pieces can be cut and temaki, a hand roll that is eaten in 2-3 bites and looks like an ice cream cone. Maki-sushi is served with soy sauce and gari.

Makisu – This object is used for making rolled sushi. A makisu is a mat from bamboo sticks that are tied together with thread. This is an essential tool in making rolled sushi.

Masago (smelt roe) – Masago are small, orange flying-fish eggs, a true delicacy in Japan. Masago can be prepared as nigiri-sushi gunkan or maki-sushi and is often used to garnish the outside of hand rolls. Masago is closely related to tobiko, flying-fish roe, and although it is somewhat lighter in color, it has the same salty taste and firm bite.

Nigiri-sushi or nigiri-zushi – Nigiri-sushi means "pressed with the hand." It is a piece of cooked or raw fish that is placed diagonally over a ball of rice. The ingredients are then carefully pressed together. Fish roe is also used for nigiri-sushi, with a strip of seaweed holding everything together. Nigiri-sushi is often served with wasabi and should be dipped in soy sauce.

Sake (salmon) – Salmon is a very popular type of sushi, easy to recognize by its bright orange color. It tastes sweet and soft. Salmon is never served raw in sushi bars; the fish is usually first smoked lightly, then conserved for a number of days in salt and sugar, then served.

Sashimi – Sashimi means "raw fish." Sashimi is served without rice, but is often dipped in soy sauce and eaten with wasabi and ginger. Sashimi is usually eaten at the beginning of the meal, before the sushi.

Sushi – Japanese main course in which rice scented with vinegar is combined with fish. Sushi is available in many forms and can be eaten with chopsticks or with the hands. The most popular types of sushi are nigiri-sushi (handmade sushi) and maki-sushi (sushi rolled with a bamboo mat).

Suzuki (sea bass) – Japanese fish with shiny, white meat and a mild taste. The fish is sometimes served as sashimi called suzuki usu zukuri.

Tako (octopus) – The tako can be recognized by its tentacles: the arms of the octopus are the most edible part of the body. Tako is always cooked before serving, softening the meat and making it somewhat firmer and subtler in taste.

Tekka-maki – A raw tuna-and-rice roll. The name tekka refers to the casinos in Japan where this snack is served at the gambling table to eat with the hands.

Unagi (freshwater eel) – Unagi looks like anago (conger eel) in terms of color and taste. However, it is not cooked first, but broiled and glazed with a mixture of soy sauce, sugar, and eel broth. The sauce makes the taste sweet and rich. Unagi should be eaten without dipping sauce.

Uni (sea urchin) – Uni is worth a try for the more courageous sushi-eater. The sea urchin is considered a delicacy in many parts of the world. What are actually served are the gonads of the sea urchin. The soft texture, which is kept in place by a strip of nori, has a delicious, subtle nutty taste and is a true favorite among experienced sushi-eaters.

Wasabi (horseradish) – A pungent, green horseradish paste with a strong taste that helps to bring out the flavor of the sushi.

Index